Old, Older, Oldest

Animals That Live Long Lives

by Michael Dahl

illustrated by Brian Jensen

PICTURE WINDOW BOOKS
Minneapolis, Minnesota

Thanks to our advisers for their expertise, research, and advice:

Dr. James F. Hare, Associate Professor of Zoology
University of Manitoba
Winnipeg, Manitoba

Susan Kesselring, M.A., Literacy Educator
Rosemount-Apple Valley-Eagan (Minnesota) School District

Editorial Director: Carol Jones
Managing Editor: Catherine Neitge
Creative Director: Keith Griffin
Editor: Christianne Jones
Story Consultant: Terry Flaherty
Designer: Nathan Gassman
Production Artist: Angela Kilmer
Page Production: Picture Window Books
The illustrations in this book were created with pastels.

Picture Window Books
5115 Excelsior Boulevard, Suite 232
Minneapolis, MN 55416
877-845-8392
www.picturewindowbooks.com

Printed in the United States of America.

Library of Congress Cataloging-in-Publication Data
Dahl, Michael.
Old, older, oldest : animals that live long lives / written by
Michael Dahl ; illustrated by Brian Jensen.
p. cm. — (Animal extremes)
Includes bibliographical references and index.
ISBN 1-4048-1173-7 (hardcover)
ISBN 1-4048-1746-8 (paperback)
1. Animals—Longevity—Juvenile literature. I. Jensen, Brian, ill.
II. Title.

QP85.D34 2005
591.3'5—dc22   2005003736

Animals live everywhere. They fly over the highest mountains and dive through the deepest oceans. They run over the hottest deserts and swim in the coldest waters.

Some animals live extremely long lives. Watch the ages on the number line rise as you turn each page.

Shhhhwwwwwwww!

A dromedary camel struts through a sandstorm in Africa. It can live up to 50 years.

Can any animal live longer?

20   40   60   80   100   120   140   160

50 Years

Yes! An Asian elephant can! It can live up to 70 years. In southeast Asia, an elephant flings water across its back.

Can any animal live longer?

20   40   60   80   100   120   140   160

70 Years

Yes! The blue-fronted Amazon parrot can! It perches on a branch in a Costa Rican jungle. It can live up to 80 years.

Can any animal live longer?

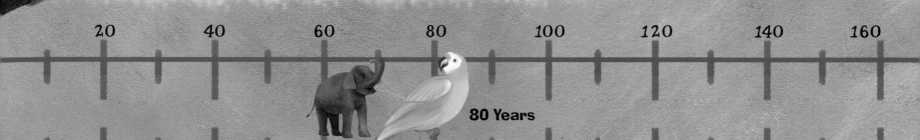

20   40   60   80   100   120   140   160

80 Years

Yes! A Moluccan cockatoo can! It can live up to 85 years. It rests in a tree in the Molucca Islands in Indonesia.

Can any animal live longer?

20   40   60   80   100   120   140   160

85 Years

Yes! A box turtle can! It burrows in mud under decaying logs in North Carolina. It can live up to 100 years.

Can any animal live longer?

20   40   60   80   100   120   140   160

100 Years

Yes! A Madagascar radiated tortoise can! It can live up to 188 years in the dry woodlands of Madagascar.

14

Can any animal
live longer?

20   40   60   80   100   120   140   160   180   200

188 Years

Yes! A bowhead whale can! It can live up to 200 years. It glides through the cold waters of the Arctic Ocean.

Can any animal live longer?

200 Years

Yes! A quahog can! This clam slowly moves through the thick mud in Rhode Island. It can live up to 225 years.

Can any animal live longer?

| 20 | 40 | 60 | 80 | 100 | 120 | 140 | 160 | 180 | 200 | 220 |

225 Years

Perhaps. Who knows what could live longer?

Extreme Fun Facts

Camels do not store water in their humps. They store fat. Baby camels don't have a hump when they are born because they don't have enough fat yet.

dromedary camel

An elephant's trunk has more than 40,000 muscles in it. A trunk is an elephant's upper lip and nose.

Asian elephant

Amazon parrots were first called Kriken, which is a version of a French word meaning "screechers."

blue-fronted Amazon parrot

Cockatoos raise their crest when alarmed. The name cockatoo comes from a Malayan word that means "big parrot."

Moluccan cockatoo

The box turtle's shell has two parts. The carapace is the top part of the shell. The plastron is the lower part of the shell. The two parts are connected with a hinge.

box turtle

Madagascar radiated tortoise

Madagascar radiated tortoises can store food and water so well that they can go without eating or drinking for up to one year.

bowhead whale

Female bowhead whales are bigger than males. The females weigh between 80 and 110 tons (72 and 99 metric tons).

quahog

A quahog's age can be figured out by counting the rings on its shell. As quahogs get older, they grow more slowly. The growth rings get very close together and difficult to count accurately.

Glossary

burrow—*to dig a hole in the ground*

crest—*long feathers on a bird's head*

decay—*to rot slowly*

perch—*to sit or rest*

sandstorm—*a wind storm that blows sand around*

woodlands—*land covered with trees*

To Learn More

At the Library

Klein, Leonore. *Old, Older, Oldest*. New York: Hastings House, 1983.

Silverstein, Alvin. *Nature's Champions: The Biggest, the Fastest, the Best*. Mineola, N.Y.: Dover Publications, 2003.

Taylor, David. *The Long Lived and Short Lived Animal Book*. Austin, Texas: Raintree Steck-Vaughn, 1996.

On the Web

FactHound offers a safe, fun way to find Web sites related to this book. All of the sites on FactHound have been researched by our staff.

1. Visit *www.facthound.com*

2. Type in this special code: 1404811737

3. Click on the FETCH IT button.

Your trusty FactHound will fetch the best sites for you!

Index

Look for all of the books in the Animal Extremes series:

Cold, Colder, Coldest: *Animals That Adapt to Cold Weather*

Deep, Deeper, Deepest: *Animals That Go to Great Depths*

Fast, Faster, Fastest: *Animals That Move at Great Speeds*

High, Higher, Highest: *Animals That Go to Great Heights*

Hot, Hotter, Hottest: *Animals That Adapt to Great Heat*

Old, Older, Oldest: *Animals That Live Long Lives*